Contents

Written by Jillian Powell

Collins

Going for gold

The first modern Olympic Games were held in Athens, Greece, in 1896. American James Connolly was the first medal winner.

The first champions' medals were not gold but silver!

The first Winter Olympics were in 1924.

Since then, many of the world's top athletes have gone for Olympic gold.

But some have to fight harder than most to become Olympic **champions**.

Hard times

The 1936 Olympics were held in Germany. The German leader Adolf Hitler was a **Nazi**. He believed that the white German people were better than all others.

Adolf Hitler in the crowd at the Berlin Olympics in 1936

4

A German athlete salutes the Nazi party.

He didn't even want black athletes to take part in the Olympics.

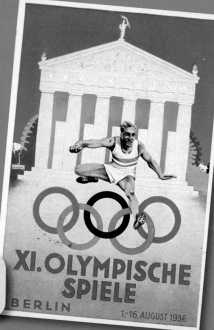

poster for the Berlin Olympics

XI. OLYMPISCHE SPIELE
BERLIN
1.-16. AUGUST 1936

5

This man showed that black athletes could be great champions. He broke 11 Olympic records at the Berlin Games and won four gold medals.

Brave beginners

These men were the first to come from a hot, sunny country to **compete** in a snow sport. At home, they had to practise on tracks and sandy beaches.

➤➤➤ *the Jamaican bobsled team*

the Jamaican team at the 1988
Winter Olympics in Canada

They had to borrow bobsleds from other teams for the Winter Olympics. They crashed on a run, but walked on to the finish line as the crowd cheered.

The Jamaican bobsled team crashed on the bend.

Battling illness

This man won an Olympic medal after having a life-saving operation. He needed a new liver to keep him alive.

Chris Klug

In 2000 he went into hospital for an **operation** to replace his liver. Less than two years later he won a bronze medal for snowboarding at the Winter Olympics.

Winning wheels

This woman was born with a **disability** which meant she couldn't walk or run. Being in a wheelchair didn't stop her becoming a great athlete and champion.

Tanni Grey-Thompson

She entered her first wheelchair race when she was 13 and won her first medal in the **Paralympic** Games six years later.

Tanni Grey-Thompson races to the finish in her orange wheelchair.

She had to stop training to have an operation on her **spine**, but went on to win four gold medals in the 1992 games.

She took part in five Paralympic Games and won a total of 16 medals, including 11 golds.

Future champions

Every Olympic Games brings new champions. All have trained hard and some have overcome illness, disability or **prejudice** to win gold.

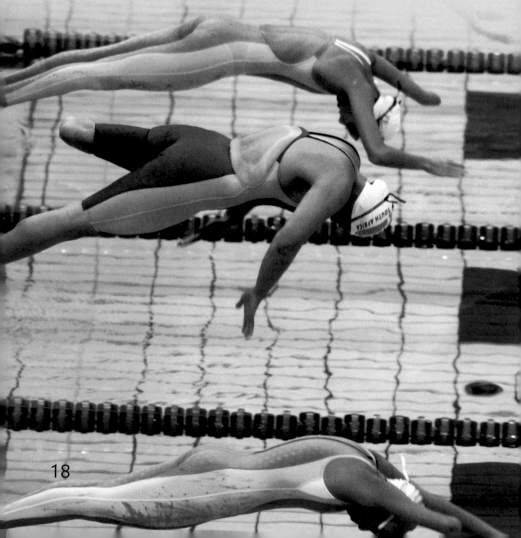

There'll be many more
Olympic heroes in the future!

Glossary

bobsled a sledge used for racing over snow and ice

champions people who have won in a competition

compete take part in a competition

disability something that limits ability of mind or body

operation medical treatment by a surgeon

Nazi a German political party led by Adolf Hitler from 1933–45

spine the bone in your back

Paralympic Olympic Games for athletes with disabilities

prejudice unfair feelings or opinions

Index

Olympic heroes – their challenges

	Name
	Jesse Owens
	Jamaican bobsled team
	Chris Klug
	Tanni-Grey Thompson

Problem	Success
black athletes not welcome at the Berlin Olympics	Olympic Gold
grew up without snow	a brave attempt
needed a life-saving operation	Olympic Bronze
could not walk or run	Paralympic Gold

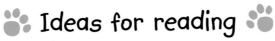

Ideas for reading

Written by Clare Dowdall BA(Ed), MA(Ed)
Lecturer and Primary Literacy Consultant

Learning objectives: apply phonic knowledge and skills as the prime approach to reading and spelling unfamiliar words that are not completely decodable; read more challenging texts which can be decoded using acquired phonic knowledge and skills along with automatic recognition of high frequency words; find specific information in simple texts; comment on events, characters and ideas, making imaginative links to their own experiences

Curriculum links: P.E.; Games activities; Citizenship; Choices

High frequency words: could, be

Interest words: Olympic heroes, bobsled, champions, compete, disability, operation, Nazi, spine, Paralympic, prejudice

Word count: 364

Resources: whiteboard

Getting started

- Ask children to discuss what they know about the Olympic games, then read the title and blurb with the children.

- Look at the photos on the cover. Ask children to describe what the man is doing, and what they think makes him an Olympic hero. Support them to make meaning and use interesting vocabulary, and write their ideas on a whiteboard.

- Read through the interest words together, helping children to identify the phonemes and to practise blending to read words such as *O-l-y-m-p-i-c*.

Reading and responding

- Walk through the book with the children. Identify the different features of an information book, e.g. photographs, information boxes, emboldened words, glossary and index and discuss how they are used.